Life's Pitfalls

Teddy Andrew Mulenga MD (Crimea)

DEDICATION

This little book I dedicate to my woman Kasonu Chizombu, my niece Mpundu, my brother Emilio, my friend Grable Mwikisa, Lulu Mwikisa, Mr and the tragically departed , Mrs. Mwanza, Mr and Mrs Mbumwae. Mrs Mwala, the engineer Mr. Mumba, Dr. Mataa Lisulo, Mr. Mathews Pikiti, my child hood friend Alick Chanda and many other close people who have gone to prepare the gates of heaven for us.

Above all my thanks goes to my prematurely departed sister Martha and my mother Bana Mikusao whose patience , guidance and self sacrifice made it easier for me to see the light of day. And of course I cannot forget the ever workaholic young sister Maggie.

CONTENTS

ACKNOWLEDGMENTS

In this my second book I should sincerely thank all my family members from whom I borrowed good wisdom of taking life not too seriously, many of which have been like props in my collection of Life's pit falls. Without us having fallen into some ditches, I could not be writing this book today. The list is long but notables are my brother Nkole and Emilio, my elder sister Martha, my nieces Masiya. Pipi. Cynthia, Sibeso, my nephew , my US based nephew Innocent , my name sake nephew Mulenga and grand child Yende, my own son Mambo, and my daughter Dr.Mwango Juliet Mulenga.It is through their tribulations in life that I was able to pin down these pit falls and put them down into a larger warning disks for myself and other people to learn from. Each one of these people, have had to fall and rise again. I am but a tax collector of the practical lessons gained from their lives. And the only difference is that I have the time and ability to pen them down.

I cannot but mention the wealth of knowledge I have personally gained from my nephews from another mother.John ,Janet,Joan,and Jean Mwanza whose *never say die* attitude in dodging the bombs life throws at us, has been a great inspiration to me and my other relatives and those that have had the benefit of knowing them.

PREFACE

The best teacher of life is life itself. My son told me the other day that one can make a bomb from the internet. I agree with him, but I also reminded him that, that can not make you into a soldier! Nothing beats experience.

By any standards this is a pretty small little book. If you are allergic to reading, this is a good way to get over your problem. It won't take you more than an hour's of reading, but the worth of knowledge will leave in you for ever. Just give it a try. You might just learn a thing or two and for the price of less than the cost of your pizza or a visit to your hair dresser!

In writing this small book I have no illusions to pretend to cover all the pitfalls of life. You, dear reader, have had and will have to face many challenges in life. I have just scratched the surface with the hope that the little warnings in this book will save you or your children, your friends or grand children just a bit of time in experimenting all before coming to truth.

Life's pitfalls are a glance backwards into reality. It's a reality check, so to say. This is a closer look at how life ought to be lived. But it's not a book of regrets. It's a book of lessons learnt by falling into ditches and getting out. When writing this book, I don't for one moment claim to have all the answers to life. Many of the pitfalls you will read here will to some appear pure common sense, but I also know that even common sense is a product of experience, and may not be so common after all Sometimes one needs to fall into a ditch for one to realize how deep it is. You will be lucky if one can point out the ditch before you fall into it head first! If by going through this book a life will be changed, even if its one, then it would have achieved its aim. We all learn from mistakes, what is bad is to repeat them or to ignore the warnings. Warning signs on the high way are not for decorations; they may save a life!

In life we ought to learn from one another. Every body has something he can teach the other, regardless of age, gender, and profession. It's only a fool that looks down on others. The only thing that differentiates us is that, others are prepared to document things, while the earth continues to spin on its axis. Do not be afraid to share your experiences. The biggest critics I know are those who sit on the side lines, afraid to take the plunge.

I am not a life coach, for I have always hated labels, especially if they are not earned. I believe the mind of a person must be able to explore without regard to artificial labels. A life coach is one who claims to know it all, who has answers to every situation in life. I don't, and don't think any one has, either. But some things I know and some things you know. This little book is a treatise on sharing with you just part of the cake of life, not all. Much of what you are about to read is part of personal experience, part of experiences of those that have been close to me and of course, part of it from observations of successful and unsuccessful people, coupled with a bit of research here and there. By all means don't treat what will follow in this book as gospel truth for sometimes circumstances do change. Always be aware that truth is relative to time and space. Nothing is cast in stone. This as it may be, human nature has been well studied and some things we simply have to agree upon. You can't deny that the brain is the citadel of your body for instance; it's the commander in chief of all military operations in your body! Neither am I claiming to discover America, old Columbus did that for us. Am told it's in the Western hemisphere, I checked it up in an atlas and its true! Isn't that amazing? I didn't have to grapple in the dark for answers, for some one took the trouble to reveal the secret!

Don't be afraid to be different.Dont be afraid to differ with people.Dont expect the world to agree with you. If that happens, chances are, you have nothing worth while to offer. When every body agrees with you, reexamine your views. Non conformity has been, through the better part of history, the mother of progress.

Life's pitfalls are an attempt at warning those who do not care to respect experience. It's an affirmation of the views of those that are pragmatic. Life's pitfalls might just save that child from falling into common pot holes along his or her journey. Sometimes, I think that if our parents were all able to document life's pitfalls, we would be better children. The world being how it is, not all of us are lucky enough to have living parents. As a result, many a child out there comes to avoid pit falls in their lives the hard way round, after falling into ditches! Often we see peer pressure being the locomotive of some children's life decisions. Others stumble upon truth through trial and error, which is the harder way to learn.

Neither you nor I can change the world entirely, but it is my sincere prayer that even if one life gets to be changed for the better by reading this small book, then God bless!

1 READING

Since you can see these words, what better way to start the journey than to discuss reading? We are living in funny times, times that seem to be putting the TV screen above everything else. The value of a good book is slowly being eroded especially in our developing countries. I never heard of a nation that fought high illiteracy levels by TV. Libraries have been left to die an agonizing death. In most African countries, television and radio stations are left to mushroom with impunity. Our nations are suffering from a poor reading culture among their citizens.

The value of a good book in shaping human consciousness can not be over emphasized. A person that picks up a good book is transformed at the end of the book. The person travels with the author on an uninterrupted journey. This journey, when reading a book, can be stopped for breaks at any time. This journey can be relieved simply by turning a page back wards .A good book is an excursion into the author's deepest thoughts; what we can't say about an hour's TV or radio programme .Some people's reading is simply a glance at a popular newspaper head line. A person that does not value books has a very myopic view of the world, of other people's cultures and belief systems. It is also widely accepted that a society without its own written word is a backward society. A society that has no alphabet of its own has rarely got anything to sell to the world.

The last time I checked, you wouldn't rewind a television broadcast, not unless you were recording it. Nothing beats the value of a well stocked personal library. And for me, I go for a book because you can do all sorts of things with it. You can highlight the sentences or whole paragraphs; you can underline important facts to refer back later. Or tear off some pages, if you so wish!

Thanks to technology, we now have e- books on line; they are still books, anyway. It also undisputed fact that one who reads a lot of English books, for example, sooner than later, becomes good in the language and has a bigger chance of becoming a writer compared to the TV fanatic.

I myself am a living legend of what reading can do .In my child hood, our library was a good 1 hr's walk from my village, yet somehow, I used to go borrow books from it. A practice I borrowed from my elder sister Martha, who was doing secondary school then. Soon I noticed a vast improvement in my reading and writing skills. I carried this love for books to secondary school that I could even read the famous James Hadley Chase of those days, in just under two days per book. I noticed a tremendous change in my school reading and writing skills. By the time I was doing form four or what is sometimes called grade 11, I was attempting to write fiction books, as a result. Though today I have gravitated away from writing fiction books, for life is real, it's no fiction! Not that I have any thing against fiction readers.

You can never go wrong with reading. For God's sake, read something and you will see what I am talking about. Show me one writer that was not an avid reader and I promise to show you a donkey grazing in your bedroom! A nation that does not nurture the need for its citizens to read is a dead one .A family that has no reading culture is a boring entity. A parent that does not encourage a reading culture among his or her children is as good as a dead one. Reading not only broadens one's perspective in life but cultivates a rich mine field of knowledge. It's through reading, you remember, I was reminded of how one can make a bomb! You can even learn to pilot a DC 10 Air craft just from reading alone! In short, you can pretty become a better farmer just by reading. Even a professor that shuns reading is sooner over taken by those who read, simply because, those who read become by implication, better writers, and better researchers. There is no single successful country that does not encourage reading. And only nations with an alphabet of their own have progressed in history.

If I had my way, I would build you a huge library than a stadium or a boxing ring; I would pay the librarian better than the boxing promoter or football coach. But I don't have my way, so will have to put up with the nonsense. It is a sad thing that some people's idea of reading ends up by their noses, with the daily newspaper!

So next time you think of rushing to a football match. Just think about when was the last time you held a book!

The greatest harm, especially a child can bring upon one self, is to spend hrs upon hrs in front of a TV screen. The greatest good one can bring upon them selves is to read a few pages of a good book each day. With each page one reads the mind is enriched. Let me leave you with the thought below:

" Read every day something no one is reading. Think something no one is thinking. It is bad for the mind to be always a part of unanimity."- Christopher Morley

2 EDUCATION

Perhaps I should have titled this chapter knowledge, a product of education. Simply because knowledge is education and education is knowledge. You can loose all the riches you have, all the gadgets, but you cannot loose education. No one can steal knowledge from you. With education or knowledge it is possible to get back that which one has lost. This is one property even the greatest bandit has yet to figure out how to steal from some one else. The greatest gift a parent can shower upon his or her child is education and it's off shoot of knowledge. Education opens doors to the world. Education is the greatest key to human development. Some people erroneously think religion is the greatest gift you can give to a child but an ignorant believer is not worth it at all. For even to study the Koran or Bible one needs education first.

I have heard of politicians who lament at the high cost of universal free education in their nations. But I dare them to try ignorance!

I believe that even a fool will agree on the benefits of education above everything else, so I won't labour the point. In fact, what seems to be in dispute is how to provide this education to the vast majority of the population in a given a nation: not its merit. There is no better tool than education is for leveling the ground between different classes of society.

I speak of education in this chapter to denote both informal and formal education. For education is nothing more other than a process by which new knowledge is gained. In my view effective education should involve al the three H's- the head, the heart and the hands. Education that involves only one aspect of these H's is often lopsided. I have to meet a parent who would not want their child to be educated.

What message are we sending out there when we reward the boxer than the teacher, than the librarian? Or for that matter the politician than the educationalist? The world seems to have agreed on the value of education but the world seems to be dong exactly the opposite.

3 TEENAGE PREGNANCY

In Zambia today close to 15 000 teenagers get pregnant every year. At one school in the Western part of the country more than 30 pupils were found pregnant at a go. In 2014, TV showed a picture of a 10 year old that had become pregnant in a shanty compound of the city of Ndola. Doctors it was reported were rightly planning to deliver her by caesarian section. Teenage pregnancy is a tragedy spreading among most of the African countries, not only Zambia.

A Teenager who gets pregnant invariably faces a greater risk associated with pregnancy. The body of a teenager is not fully developed to carry a pregnancy and deliver without risks. These kids often shy away from ante natal follow ups. They are at a greater risk of developing high blood pressure. And high blood pressure in pregnancy is a major cause of maternal death in our developing countries.

Early sexual activity in a child predisposes the child to acquiring the dreaded human papilloma virus that later in life may lead to the emergency of cervical cancer. Not to talk of the possibility of getting infected with HIV and other sexually transmitted infections.

When one looks at the above it becomes apparent that a country that has resolved to introduce giving of maternity leave to pregnant teenagers has only looked at one aspect of the problem of educating the girl child. Re-entry policy as it is called could be an honourable policy but it alone cannot solve the ballooning problems associated with teenage pregnancies. A mother child even when goes back to school assumes a greater load on society to bring forth her child. Children of girl mothers invariably are likely to be street kids.   Neither does re-entry policy protect the young body from the medical dangers associated with an early pregnancy and delivery process.

My view is that the solution of teenage pregnancy lies in solving the high poverty levels prevalent in our countries. Unfortunately though, poverty can never be solved in a day. No wonder we have some NGO's advocating for provision of condoms in schools. This view seems to be an admission of failure in my understanding. A Society that opts for provision of condoms in schools in my view has simply admitted defeat. Neither does the condoms availability lead to use in a young person. I still think that society should not turn schools into child production centres.Abstinence is the song to sing till it sinks into the young mind. This is not a religious view it's simply pragmatism. I also think that Governments must in the interim invest greatly in provision of boarding facilities for young people. Young girls left to rent single quarters away from school are more at risk of being exploited. This is how I see the way to avoid the pit falls of teenage pregnancy. For those advocating for provision of condoms in schools, I always have only one challenge-Let them pack condoms in their childrens' lunch boxes!

Let me say it again. Abstinence is the best contraceptive ever discovered by mankind. For those who don't agree with this approach, could they say there were fewer pregnancies in teens 20 years ago because of availability of condoms in schools? Some thing is just wrong in the way we are going about solving this problem. In my view an NGO run by a school drop out cannot provide sensible answers to this problem. Forgive my abrasiveness if you aren't a school drop out!

4 STUDY

Schools teach material, but schools do not teach how to retain that which they churn out. Many a child has failed not because they are not taught but because they didn't know how to retain that which they are taught. Some lucky children simply come to acquire proper studying methods by simple trial and error. I look forward to a day when children will have guidance in study methodology on the same scale that career and moral education is being approached. In Botswana, all schools teach what they call guidance and counseling, but even them study methodology is not among the subjects. Yet society can not argue with me that the basis of success lies in teaching the child early in life proper studying techniques.

I am neither a teacher nor qualified educationalist but I have done a lot of research on this topic. Here, I will just share some little tips in study techniques that are bound to make a change in retention of taught material. For a little bit more down to earth detail read the concerned chapter in my first book The Sceptic.

First and foremost, you need to take notes whenever you are studying any material. Proper upright posture is a must, unless one is reading a poem or novel for enjoyment. Do not study while lying in bed, for you are simply sending wrong messages to your mind that it is time to sleep. Proper propped up position ensures good Oxygen intake to your brain. Note taking engages the visual capacities of your brain to come into play. Do not fear to underline and high light texts. High lighting has been greatly used by those wanting to remember Bible verses. You may like wise write notes, short notes by the margins of text books or exercise books. You have to align your audio to your video.

If you are a college or university student taking lecture notes, remember to indent your notes to kill the monotony. Use Mind maps if you know what they are. Use different coloured pens or pencils to emphasize your ideas. Use any funny drawing that your mind comes across to make associations with your material. Mnemonics may become handy if you are imaginative enough. The mind remembers better funny striking stuff. If your lecturer is one of those that come with plenty of written notes to deliver their lectures consider missing their lectures to spend your time making your own notes in the library. It's a pity that some lecturers demonstrate their ignorance of material by coming with huge notes. The irony is, if they can hardly remember their material without notes, how can you? Avoid such shallow minds, they are a bore!

Do not spend sleepless nights studying. Your memory will fail you at the crucial moment. Have enough rest. Sleep well, to a minimum of six hours. The brain needs rest. Don't push it too far.

Breaks of 15 minutes are a must when studying material. Walk about or listen to some light music. Take a cup of tea or coffee. Coffee is a stimulant because it contains caffeine. But do not depend on it too much, as caffeine can be addictive. This can result in an ever increasing demand in quantity to keep you awake. Keep away from commercial pills as stimulants, they are likely to keep you awake much longer when your brain will need to recharge. To this category I put Red bull.

The greatest mistake pupils make in studying is to follow the band wagon. If you have your friends waking up in the middle of the night to study, leave them alone. Keep to your schedule. Consistence with proper rest is the mother of success.

How long should you keep at study? A maximum of two hrs a session might be adequate, interspaced with short rest periods. Concentrate on the harder material when you are all fresh, leave the easy part towards the end.

Back ground soft music if you are not in the Library can some times be beneficial. Avoid loud music that may distract you and those close by.

Always strive to get a quick over view of the material you want to study. Look at the contents. Read the summary. Flip through the inside of the book quickly to see the relevance of the material you intend to study. It does not pay to spend valuable time on less important material that you realize to be useless only at the end of your session.

It is not my intention to go through all the nuances of successive study techniques, but my point is to campaign for it to become a subject in student life. This way the unnecessary ditch of failing can be avoided in most cases.

5 GAMBLING

Who doesn't want to be rich? Having plenty of money is not a prerequisite to happiness but try poorness! Like it or not the world revolves around money. Some body has already written the script for us. Money isn't going away any sooner. Even the Pope needs money! The church needs money! Every body needs money! True, money cannot buy happiness. Money can not buy health. Many people who fail to appreciate this fact end up spending valuable time and resources guarding their money. But it also true that money does solve most problems. Money becomes a problem when one gets obsessed with it. The problem is not money per say but our attitudes towards it.

Some people spend all their lives dreaming of money. I remember one miner who committed suicide after loosing all his pay in a casino chasing riches. I had to go with Police to bring down his body from a tree he used to hang himself, for us to conduct a post mortem on him.

Casinos may be great entertainment joints but you got to know how far to go. *'Pick a lot''* lotteries are great ideas but one needs to know the game of probability well. Often people who spend their earnings in gambling do not give a thought to elementary mathematics. Casinos aren't built to make you rich. Lotteries aren't devised to make you rich. No one gives out money just like that. The possibility of you guessing five right numbers out of fifty in a lottery goes into millions! Money has to be worked for; it never falls out of machines! Apparently gamblers have very little regard for mathematical principles. Some gamblers even bring God into the equation. God is often not so interested after all in throwing money out of machines! I have known people who have played lotto since they were young men and women and are now old and still keep hoping that one day it is going to happen. Many of these will carry their lotto tickets to their graves!

The problem with gambling is that it is addictive. The machines are designed in such a way that they always give you an encouragement only to hit you below the belt when the chips are down. The unfortunate thing is that even governments are encouraging gambling. Casinos are licensed by the state. Radio lotto shows are state sanctioned. Even the state wants a fast buck! What a world we are living in! In spite of you paying tax the state wants to squeeze the remainder out of you! Little wonder that miner had to end his life. Some people do not simply remember to stop digging once they fall into a ditch.

Gambling, be it private or state sponsored is a cause of a lot of misery among people. The state has a good word for it –lotto! At the end of the day the name does not change the nature of the game. In most Moslem countries state or private gambling gimmicks are not allowed. This is one good thing we should borrow from the Muslims. They may produce suicide bombers but this surely is a virtue we should all respect. There is nothing inherently good in gambling. Like the suicide victim I once '*post mortemed.*" Gambling is a social evil and must be discouraged.

Get it from me; the best gambler is one who goes there just to pass time and not to become rich. If you are not prepared to throw your money into a gulley, do not play lotto or visit casinos. The sad part of it all is that even on rare occasions that you have a winner, its easy come easy go. I have yet to meet a millionaire from gambling. Money is lost as soon as it is won. It's a pitfall that needs to be avoided. The only better gambler is a dead one!

6 MARRIAGE

This is one pitfall that is a hand full. There is no single prescription for a successful marriage. You won't find it in the scriptures .You won't find it in some manual out there. If the men of God are claiming to have found the answer, just point to the high divorce rates among religious people. If you have your parents still living and still together, chances are that they may have found the formula. Ask them and learn from them, they have seen it all, not your counselor! They are better teachers than you and me will ever be!

In saying a few words on marriage I pray that you won't accuse me of moralizing. I have no formula either, but that does not stop one at searching for the right answers to successful marriages. What makes marriage a difficult thing is that it's a union of different beings with different experiences, different hopes and fears, and sometimes different aims and goals all together in life. Fortunately, though among the so many failures there are few good successful endings. It is these few successful marriages that we should draw our lessons from.

If you go into marriage for riches, chances are that when the manna stops falling, that marriage is bound to collapse. If you enter into marriage because your partner has two legs, please remember your partner might loose one leg during your life together. If you enter into marriage because of similar religious beliefs, remember people do change. Those that enter into marriages with a view of changing their partners, sooner than later, become discouraged when the script does not exactly fall into place.

Marriage is an evolutionary product that denotes bringing up of off springs as a unit, to make a much easier procreation process. I there fore laugh sometimes when I hear so called life coaches{ whatever that means} advise couples to break off regardless of the third parties – the children. A marriage that looks only at the happiness of one single partner is not worth the certificate it was written on. It pure is selfness to only think about ones happiness ignoring the fate of the by products, the children. From this view it follows that a partner that sacrifices their personal happiness for that of their children deserves some respect. Individual happiness sometimes has to be sacrificed for the good of the children; Children are the most vulnerable members in a family. So should they not have a say? Forget the culture of the Hollywood stars, like Elizabeth Taylor, who remarried a record nine times! Stick to the dictates of your culture. For this same reason marrying out side community of property is in my view rather a stupid idea, sorry for the strong words.

Successful couples are ones who find time together. If your partner enjoys going out and wishes you to remain at home all alone, such a partnership is bound to fail. Go out together or sit at home both of you. What is right for the man should be right for the woman too.

Make time together to eat out with your children. Travel together, visit theme parks, game parks and any tourist places of interest. If church is an important thing in your lives go there together. Attend sports functions together even if your interests may not exactly coincide. A successful marriage denotes loosing some and winning some, you can't have it all. No body said life was fair!

Find time for your children's school activities even if they may appear rather childish. If your child is a swimmer or chess player or is in drama, find time to attend the functions. Of course work demands may just make the other partner unable to fulfill these demands, bur at least one of you should be able to take the front seat. And please take keen interest in your child's school books and home work. Like wise, take keen interest in your partner's professional life. Take time to listen to your partner's professional battles.

Conflicts will always be there. That's part of human nature. What is important is to have tolerance and a listening ear. Always try to fit in the shoes of your partner and see how it feels. Most important of all, never resolve sensitive issues in the presence of your children. It creates a psychological trauma that is difficult to resolve later. After all, in the eyes of the growing child, you are both film stars!

Above all, when the going gets tough do not abandon your partner, keeping in mind your vows of '' *for better and for worse.* ''

7 FUNERAL

There are two important dates for any human, the day of birth and the day of death. One of these dates is completely oblivious to the concerned. One of these dates the concerned is present during celebrations, the other is celebrated without the owner's presence.

Funerals especially in Africa are most often than not pitfalls. There is so much unwarranted spending that results in many a family experiencing a double loss. In my first book The Sceptic, I alluded to the cries of former President of Botswana, Mr. Festus Mogae, when he bemoaned the excessive spending at funerals in his country of Botswana. At such funerals apart from costly caskets, one or two beasts are often slaughtered, with the whole spectacle turning into a feeding frenzy for the community. I think Festus had a point. But his people never listened to his wise counsel.

Many dead people if they could just see what spending is associated with their burial would without doubt protest. But as it is, the dead tell no tales. Let's take a leaf from the Muslims who bury their dead within 24 hrs and only use the simplest of covers, sometimes just a white bed sheet. The person is dead any way; there is no point in dramatizing issues. The family one leaves behind will need all the finances that are wasted on grandiose funerals.

The way I see it, is like, the alive are simply playing to the gallery. The flashy expensive caskets are more a statement to those seeing than the claimed respect to the dead. No one who has left dependants behind would wish them to further slide into poverty, all in the name of sending one in style. Wishes of the departed are with impunity ignored all in the name of showing off to the mourners. At some funerals thousands of people are fed who, in effect, do not mean a thing to the departed, both before and after burial. Thousands of cash are spent that would best be given to the dependants one leaves behind. Some relatives behave as though the departed is feeling the drama surrounding one's funeral.

I don't know about other tribes. But am also reminded of a very irritating practice among the Bemba of Northern Zambia, which in my view, smacks of nothing but property grabbing. This is the so called " *isambo lya mfwa.*" This is a practice where relatives, even distant ones, behave like wolves just a day after burial; where by, clothes of the deceased are brought out for the living to share. This is a practice that leaves the closest relatives with a bitter taste in their mouths. Distant relatives of the deceased swam like bees upon the clothes of the departed and shortly after wards just vanish in thin air, sometimes not even giving a thought to the spouse or children left behind by the departed. It is a practice the Bembas must just consider discarding. It is pure greed, it stinks! And perhaps its time we started to write and respect wills.

Coming back to the spending at funerals, it should be humble! Its time we stopped playing to the gallery. In my view a funeral should just be a funeral and not be used to show off to the rest of society with grandiose performances and unwarranted spending.

The dead tell no tales!

8 WEDDING

I have never seen a tombstone that says' *Here lies so and so who was born on ...and wed on......*". What I have written above about funerals goes also for weddings. At the risk of sounding repetitive let us sing the song again. Repetition is the mother of learning, so they say.

The spending that accompanies the modern wedding leaves much to be desired. The young couple getting married often forgets that there is life after the wedding. Limousines are ordered, expensive hotels booked, expensive menu is ordered, coupled with an expensive band. Not to mention expensive clothes for the bride and bride groom, all the way to the best men and women. It's like someone is marrying the whole world! A wedding is turned into a circus show than a celebration of the union of two people.

At the end of it all, the young couple goes and down loads their photos onto face book just to make a statement. When the dust has settled, the young couple finds there is life to lead after all. Often they are in debt to their chins. The blame games start, and before you sneeze, the marriage is on the rocks. Unless one is a Bill Gates, or a Hollywood star, one needs to play it cool! Need I say more on this one?

I have met couples who jump into marriage and wedding without even having a proper home where the couple are supposed to stay, unless one is forced to marry because of unplanned pregnancy this rush is a stupid thing to do. Its goes without saying that one need have an independent secure home before one commits. The idea that things will sort themselves after the wedding is misplaced thinking. Things never sort themselves. You need to plan .Why would one rush into marriage and a lavish wedding ceremony when one is staying in servant's quarter. This is a way on inversing priorities. Such marriages eventually collapse when reality starts to bite. That there are few success stories in spite of the above is no reason to make one to dive into a swimming pool without disrobing.

The other tragedy I have seen is women who move in into a man's house without officially getting married to them, they cook and wash clothes for their men. Eventually such women do loose the men, they simply unknowingly extinguish the passion before the man has committed. A woman should be scarce but available; a woman should keep the fire burning till commitment is achieved, in this case marriage.

9 CREDIT CARDS

Remember this; banks do not throw around money! Banks are in it not for you. Do not ever spend that which is not yours. The best one should have is a debit card. That's your money. Credit cards are the sure way of jumping into debt head down. Credits cards are designed in a way that will forever leave you in debt. It's a vicious circle that has very unpleasant ending. The moment you commit your self to use of credit cards, you are in deep waters. Even when you decide to close your credit account, you will be taken from pillar to pillar. Banks do not steal from you, there are in to make profit. The seemingly unlimited spending power that a credit card gives you is a smokes screen. The problem with credit cards is they will encourage you to buy that which you really do not need. In a way there are worse than loans, for loans have a timeline. A credit card will forever leave you in perpetual debt.

In developed countries credit cards seem to be a must have phenomenon. In Africa however, its use is wide spread in most Arab countries, RSA, Namibia and Botswana. It's amazing how some families go shopping for clothes in these countries without any real money in their bank accounts, only to end up in perpetual indebtness.Credit cards in my views are only profitable to the banks and not individuals. Zambian banks have not gotten on the band wagon yet, but it's a matter of time. The banks will never tell you the bare truth; it's not in their interests. Am pretty sure your bank manager will mark me enemy number one, but I wouldn't care less. Let truth be told!

Of course if you are a fanatic of online shopping credit cards are indespensible.My only concern is that credit cards encourage people to spend that which they do not have. Believe me, the African is one big failure at managing invisible money! In this the African has a long long way to go.

No, go for a debit card! Leave credit cards to millionaires to play with, not you and me!

10 ALCOHOL

Let's face it; alcohol is not a bad thing inherently. In fact even water can kill you! The noise you hear about alcohol drinking being a sin is all a hip of clever nonsense. Even Christ did make wine at one time, and wine is even much stronger than beer. It's what you do after drinking that makes the difference. I have had the opportunity to see Catholic and Anglican fathers take beer. Drink as some of these religious leaders may, they do not take it in excess. As I said earlier, if you took too much water, doctors will tell you, you can die from water intoxication! Believe me, I have done research! A person that never flies will never die in a plane crush! A person that never climbs trees will not fall from one!

What we cannot quarrel about is that any thing done in excess is bad. Alcohol is a drug that when misused can kill off your liver, and brain cells and many other organs. Alcohol for the under age or the pregnant mother is especially dangerous. Alcohol especially the stronger brands can be very damaging to the human body. Alcohol when it is over used can be rather addictive, not to talk of the social disturbances it often induces among families and society at large.

Realizing the dangers of alcohol, some political leaders have gone to extremes to control its use. Kenneth Kaunda of Zambia once resigned his presidency for as he claimed, he couldn't lead a nation of drunkards.KK was however sweet talked into rescinding his decision within 24 hrs by his colleagues.Zambians to date rank sixth in alcohol consumption in the whole world.

 President Gorbachev of the then USSR once tried to ban the sale of alcohol {Russians are well known for their vodka!].Gorbachev called it," *sukoi zakon* ", the Russian equivalent of "dry *law*".His law could not last long however, as the Russian civil service almost went without salaries in a period of a month. He quickly relented. I remember this drama as it happened during my student life their. At least the Russians make it a point never to take their vodka on empty stomachs, vodka being a potent 70% strong spirit.

So next time you start wondering why alcohol seems to hold its day, remember the huge amounts of money that the industry churns out to state coffers in form of taxes. Apparently health concerns can always be over ridden! This scenario holds true in all the countries. The world is not such a sober place after all!

If you are lucky enough not to be attracted to alcohol consumption, please don't even dream about it. No body ever died out of not drinking. It's not food at all!

11 SMOKING

There are many habits that are difficult to defend. Smoking is perhaps is the most intriguing of them all. There isn't one good thing one can say about this pitfall, other than that it is a million dollar industry. Indeed, on these earth men that can claim not to have had an occasional pull on the cancer stick can fit in my palm. That includes me, a doctor in this equation!

Some people claim they do smoke out of stress, though there is no medical evidence to support such claims. Smoking is the only habit no one has a sensible answer to. Ask any serious smoker why they smoke and you will give no more than a shrug! No smoker really knows why they smoke, I can bet you on this! Do me a favour ask the smokers!

Cigarettes contain the addictive drug nicotine and some rubbish respectfully called tar.Cigarrette smoking is a major cause of respiratory system cancers. Sure, not every smoker gets cancer but the danger has been well proven and documented. At one time it was established that every packet so smoked shortens one's life span by a day, everything being equal. That as it may sound scary, even women are joining the band wagon with impunity in some societies. Nicotine is so addictive that a smoker actually feels sick when its levels drop in the blood.

The other day I heard a funny argument in defense of smoking. It went something like this: When you jump into a bus, you are not assured of arriving at your destination, you might be involved in an accident, but that does not stop you from boarding the bus! It sounds good reasoning, but to jump in a rickety bus with poor wheels stands you at a greater chance to be involved in an accident. The bad wheels in this case are the cigarettes. It is not after all a good argument to justify smoking.

The other day I read that the oldest human to have lived actually smoked for a hundred years! There are always side liners in this world! That is no proof for the safety of cigarette smoking. Statistics, the stuff of numbers, are not made by single facts.

Worse still, is to smoke inside buildings or near other non smokers. Smoking is the only habit that puts other non participants at great risk, through passive smoking.

Humans are a funny lot. If all are agreed it's a cause of cancer why then not ban it? The answer is simple, smoking rakes in millions of dollars for industry. Who cares about your cancer?

12 SAVING

If you are in paid employment earning a monthly salary, this is for you. But indeed what will follow will go for self employed people as well.

Probably you may not live long enough before you hang your boots, before you retire, but saving for a rainy day is a prerequisite for success in life. The rain will surely fall one of these days! Any one earning a salary, however small can save. It only requires a bit of discipline. Saving serves three main purposes:

1. To cater for your old age. If the guy upstairs permits it.
2. To cater for your childrens' education
3. To cater for the rainy day

A rainy day may come in many forms. You can loose your job, or loose your sight or leg. Some how, human nature is such that we only think it can happen to the next folk, not us. That it may happen to the non believer, not the believer! It is myopic to only live for the moment, think of the next day even if it may never come. Open a saving's account to which you only touch in extreme needs. On this one the banks are going to give me an Oscar for campaigning on their behalf! I am not a bad chap after all, even after discouraging you not to fall for their credit card gimmicks!

How much do you need to save? Any amount. The first thing one needs to do when one gets paid is to pay themselves first. Before you pay your bills pay your self first. Put away at least 10 % of your income, then pay your bills and lastly buy your food. What will remain can then go for any other business. It's not a big deal if at the end of the day you do not have anything for entertainment. No body died from lack of it! Except of course in movies.

Now ten percent may appear small but if you keep up the practice through out your working life you will be surprised how financially independent you may become over time. I won't go through the maths of this; there is rather too much online advice and several books on this one. If you are a religious person it pays to tithe to your savings account, believe me God will be happy for your pragmatism. God does not want your stinky dollars, but of course your Pastor does!

The other beneficial effect of saving that I found out over my working life is that saving gives you a peace of mind. Saving when it becomes a habit makes you not fear sudden necessary spending, because your mind is already tuned to the fact that you are likely to recover from whatever befalls you .You are at peace because you know you can do it all over again. Millionaires haven't told us the whole truth. I never knew this either early in my youth.

Later in my working life I very much remember how I used to bail out one particular doctor who was a spending fanatic. He, in spite of getting a higher salary than me, would spend all his earnings all at once and then wait for the next pay check. This fellow often asked me where I got my money from. In his mind, he thought I had some form of external funding. My secret was not external means but simple habitual consistent saving. This wisdom I gained the had way. You have a chance, start today.

One other thing I learnt is not to wait till your salary is been increased. Money is never enough. Needs and wants are a plastic phenomenon. With money every leap has the tendency of making you change your goal posts. If you were walking to work, you start to dream about getting a bicycle; if you had a bicycle, you start thinking of buying a car. And if you had a car, you start thinking of getting a helicopter! And if you had a helicopter , you start thinking of a concorde!So this way your mind keeps telling you the big lie that you can't save for you have no disposable income remaining after your unreasonable spending. Let me say it again---money is never enough. Start to save today, even small amounts as long as you keep it. Make it a habit. You will never regret it. You will write me check one of these days for this free lesson.

13 LOANS

This is one pitfall that has a double edge to it. If you are in business take care to get a loan that you have the capacity to pay off. The best thing is to live within your means. Postpone instant gratification. Do not live out of the sweat of others. This is true for the individual as it is for a nation. A nation that wants to develop through loans from the IMF or the World Bank sooner finds itself in un ending poverty situation. The IMF or the World Bank does not throw dollars away. They are in it not for your sake but for themselves. There are always strings attached to loans. Some body's money always looks good but it has to be paid off, with interest for that matter. I get worried when I see some African countries dancing when Europe loans them money; they need to shed tears actually! Some body is gotta tell them this.

A loan that is obtained with a view to expand business is in a way a welcome thing. So long one knows how one is going to pay it off. A loan obtained for purposes of buying a car before one has his own house is a foolish venture. This is putting gratification before pragmatism, the horse before the cart.

Texas Bix Bunder once wrote that never ask a barber if you need a hair cut. In the same vein, never ask your banker if you need a loan! The interests of your banker are not your interests. Leaving off loans is not a good idea, but so is loaning out your money as well. Give it out if you don't need it! That way you won't gonna get hurt when money is not returned. This is the reason Bill Gates is the greatest philanthropist. He doesn't loan out money.

He simply gives it out.

If you are asked for loans, do not give out money you wouldn't care to loose. If you are prepared to loan out money be ready to loose it some time, or do not do it. I will keep my thoughts here as short as you should keep away from loans!

.

14 QUARELLING

Quarreling is the most unproductive venture discovered by man. You can not win an argument just to leave your friend feel like a train has just run over them. Avoid quarrels; they are a loss of valuable energy.

Am not saying you shouldn't stand for what you believe in. The truth is, you can never win an argument. Agree to disagree. Life is not a debating club! Leave the other person to think they have won. Leave the other person happier than you found them. In the end you will have saved valuable energy. Avoid putting down people so as to win an argument. In the end you create unpleasant feelings towards you that you do not need. Leave the person feeling better about themselves. You will always be assumed to be a better person. This does not mean you have to trip your self over to make another person feel happy. But do not trip him or her either.

When confronted by argumentative people, keep your cool, do not raise your voice. Explain your side of the issue soberly, without malice, you may just be wrong! Always try to fit in the other person's shoes and see how it feels; the shoes might turn out to be just too tight for you as well. Be tolerant to differing points of view, so long they aren't about to bomb you. Above all remember not to quarrel on issues of taste. It's a useless under taking; your tongue is not theirs! In questions of religious belief, remember that, we are all but products of up bringing. You could as easily be a Talban if your parents were Taliban. You could as well be a Muslim if you were born in Afghanistan. If you are lucky enough to have transcended childhood indoctrination, thank your stars for it! It could have been worse!

Whatever the situation, remember that you aren't the centre of the world. And however hopeless the other view is, remember the earth wont stop spinning, not for you, not for the other person!

15 GADGETS

Beautiful ones are not yet born!

The progress of man kind is a wonderful thing. No one can keep pace with the ever changing gadgets. You buy a cell phone today; only to change it tomorrow, for what you perceive to be a better model. You buy a car today, only to wish you had bought a different model .You get PC today only to want to change it the next day, for a better one.

Nothing wrong with changing a gadget for a better improved version but sometimes people change gadgets only for show off. Sometimes, some people go for changes for change's sake; that's when it becomes a problem. Resources that can better be used for real necessities of life are diverted to useless short term items.

As I write this in July 2014, I have with me in front of my desk a newspaper which is showing a photo of the President of Uruguay, one Jose' Mujica, standing in a hospital queue waiting to be attended to by doctors. Below the caption is more information that Mujica was living in his own small house and that he drove a 1987 Volkswagen. This surely caught my attention. This President had realized that the use of a car is to get you from point A to point B, and no more. I agree, a car should not be a moving hotel room, like we see with so many other Presidents. Of course you might argue that the shiny Limousines and Benzes we see with other heads of states have to do with security. Really? Does one have to put a whole hotel room on wheels for security?

As for cell phones, the frenzy associated with new models is shocking. One would think that the use of a cell phone should be to make phone calls, not to take snaps. If you need to take snaps why not buy a camera? Or am I going backwards into civilization? Well, my point is that you don't dress like a pauper and wave around the latest I pad; you don't starve yourself and dance around with the latest cell phone, either. Neither should one move about with the latest BMW when one has no roof above his head!

The love for gadgets must surely be well measured, after all, *beautiful ones are not yet made*!

16 TRAVELLING

Some Europeans still think that Africans are still jumping on trees. This level of ignorance about other people is sometimes shocking. Some Westerners get a shock of their lives when they land into cities like Cape Town, a city that is as beautiful as any out there. And it's in Africa! I once met Tswanas, who rarely travelled, who thought that Harare and Bulawayo were villages with no cars simply because the Zimbabweans flooded Botswana at one time when Zimbabwe was going through economic hard ships. The same untraveled Batswana could not believe the sophistication of the capital of Zambia, Lusaka, simply because they equated job seeking professionals from Zambia in their country to imply, as they boasted, that Zambians lived on" *Kapenta"* [small fishes} alone. At one time I was advised by my Botswana nurses I used to work with not to drive to Zambia with my own car, since they believed Zambia had no cars! Ignorance doesn't get much worse than this.

What about some Americans who think Mandela was the President of Africa! Or that we all speak like Shaka Zulu! And this is not from some red Indians in America but so called educated Americans! Some whites that have never travelled out of Europe still think that Africans share their bedrooms with animals! You will meet a lot of these ignorant folks all over Europe and America.

As I wrote in my first book, the Bembas of Zambia will always remind you that" *umwana ashenda atasha banyina ukunaya"* meaning a child that never travels praises his or her mother's cooking as the best. Any chance you get travel out to another country or region. Travelling simply teaches humility in people.Tavelling never fails to broaden ones own world view. It's only when the American leaves California that he or she suddenly realizes that America is not the world and that some cities in Africa can actually be so modern. Berlin in Germany is a good city but those who have visited Cape Town in South Africa will find it difficult to chose which one is the best. And only when you have seen St.Petersburg in Russia or China's Peking or Cairo in Egypt would you appreciate the beauty of this world. And only when you have visited Livingstone's Victoria Falls will you praise with reservations the Niagara Falls in USA.

You never go wrong with travelling.

17 CAREER CHOICE

You are the king of your own destiny. When making a career choice, remember, you don't owe any one any explanation about your career choice. There is no such thing as a better career. Every career is important on earth. Without a teacher you would probably not be able to read this. Without the cook you wouldn't eat. Without a street sweeper you wouldn't walk around the street. Without a doctor you wouldn't be in good health. And without the accountant you wouldn't count your coins!

When making career choice follow your passion, follow the dictates of your mind. Never chose a career because it sounds great. Successful people in the world are those who engage in activities they enjoy. Don't follow the crowd. Avoid playing to the tune of others. Nothing wrong with having role models: but your father, your mother, your relatives, or your teacher, or for that matter your spouse should not choose your career for you. It's your life not theirs at the end of it all.

What ever you chose to do, aim to do it well. Aim to learn to be the best there is in your field. And above all, work much more than you are rewarded for. Give your best in whatever you are involved in. Read what ever there is on your chosen career. Remember that learning has no end. You can learn a lot even from your juniors or children. Learning does not stop with an acquisition of your certificate or degree. Avoid high sounding titles that you haven't earned. Titles like professor, doctor, bishop, prophet, apostle, just like military ranks, must be earned before you dangle them around. Your full potential can only be realized in doing something you really enjoy doing. Never chose a career for money's sake. Money should be a consequence not an end in itself, for money can not buy happiness or health. Like I said some where in my book, rich people are not necessarily happy people. That is not to say you should be content with being poor. Some times in life its enough just to have a satisfactory life. Do not spend your life guarding your millions!

Above all, remember Maslow's hierarchy of needs- aim for food before clothes, shelter before cars, and health before prestige.

18 SPEECH MAKING

You may not be a politician, but one day you will have to be called upon to make a speech. It may be at your child's birth day party or your child's wedding party. Or perhaps it could be that you will need to make a lecture or presentation to a group of people. One thing for sure though it wont be at your funeral!

Even first time singers or actors do experience stage fright: butter- flies start to fly within your stomach. For whatever occasion standing to speak in front of crowds is bound to send shivers upon someone's spine. There are no schools out there to teach you self belief. In my student days, I often switched off following a lecturer who stood with stacks and stacks of notes before a full auditorium. I could just not imagine how a person who makes his life from lecturing would still need to stick to written notes to deliver a structured lecture. I often wondered if a lecturer who would not remember their own material should expect students to remember his material in exams.

That there   must be some form of apprehension when one stands in front of multitudes to deliver a talk is all understood. It is certainly a natural reaction of the mind to perceived stress. It is the management of this adrenalin surge that defines a successful speaker from a failure.

 Poor speech making is a pitfall that can some times wreck and destroy a politician's career. No wonder spin doctors in advanced societies are becoming a popular gang for many speech makers. One can actually make money just teaching people how to speak!

Successful speech making should start with your dress code. Dress appropriately for the occasion. One guide is to know your audience well. Understand your audience's expectations and belief systems. It does not pay for one to address a religious congregation in overalls. Those overalls would perfectly be in place when talking to mechanics or labourers.

The next thing is to remember to vary your voice. This does not mean whispering to one self, neither does it mean shouting your lungs out. Speak in order to be heard by the furthest person in your audience.

Notes can help one remember the structure of one's speech. But notes should be just that, notes! All human beings enjoy spontaneity. One need not glue their eyes to one's notes. If you have to read your speech makes at least an occasional look up to your audience. Know your material well and if need be research on your material before hand from books or on line. Do not take your listeners for dummies; some of them may well know a bit more than you! If you can, speak without notes. You are more likely to sound genuine. When I used to teach obstetrics to nurses and junior doctors I won many hearts for not using notes. I appeared to all like I knew my material very well even if some topics were rather very challenging; I never failed to capture my listener's attention. It's from this practical experience that am sharing with you these tips. Be rest assured it is not googled stuff!

Humour is a good way to create rapport; however, it must not be offensive. Remember to start your speech with something memorable, if not shocking. So goes with your ending of your speech. Leave your audience with something out of the ordinary. Above all, remember at the end of your speech, to thank your listeners for tuning onto you.

19 SMILE

He has achieved success who has lived well, laughed often and loved much- Bessie Anderson.

When every thing fails smile! In my first book, The Sceptic, I wrote a satirical piece on why I would settle for a dog any time. Dogs have a way to smile that few humans can challenge. Dogs meet us with complete acceptance: that's why I have always kept dogs from age ten. I have yet to meet a dog that does not smile on meeting its owner, and it does it simply by wagging its tail. As Dr. David Lieberman in his book *"Getting any one to like you"* emphasized, *"if you have no tail to wag, then smile!"*

When you meet a person, first impressions do count a lot. Smiling has the magic of melting ice. Your smile denotes that you have accepted the other person; and who doesn't want to feel accepted? Absence of a smile on your face denotes unhappiness. And that's a good put off when meeting people, especially for the first time.

Most people erroneously feel that putting on a stiff upper lip like the British Monarchy is the way to send a message of confidence in themselves. The truth is, don't take your self too seriously; laugh and smile at your self and you will get people to appreciate your presence better. Life is not a world war. In fact; science teaches us that it takes much more effort to maintain a sad face than maintain a smile.

Look at good singers; they are always smiling as they sing. Even a smiling sales person is bound to make more sales than one with a heavy face. A smiling politician is much more believable even when he or she is talking crap.

20 CONVERSATION

We all want to be heard. It's a great pitfall in life if you only want to be heard. The greatest conversationalists on this earth are those who take time to listen. Silence is the biggest argument ever created to dispute. Say little, but something. Its only when a fish opens its mouth that it is caught!

Let us take a leaf from nature; our mouths are meant to shut, our ears aren't. And remember again that, *it is only when a fish opens its mouth that it is caught*. Poorly chosen words can be very devastating, as devastating as an atomic weapon. As one wise saying goes, *"no man —made weapon has been devised as lethal, potent or dangerous as words wrongly used.'*

For Christian believers, you will find a lot of wise sayings in the book of Proverbs to do with the power of words. I find this book in the Bible to contain a lot of wisdom, much that cannot be said about some big chunks of the Old Testament sayings, for instance. To this rubbish damp is the Old Testament writing that says work on Sabbath is punishable by death! Even picking sticks! Listen to Jesus, work if you have to, on Sabbath, it's no sin. Jesus was one clever wise man!

When you are in a conversation remember to do more listening than talking. Verbal diarrhea can be very irritating, not every body moves with a tissue paper! The other thing psychologists will tell you is, never to engage in any conversation with wrong premises or starting points. Such conversations will tend to put you on the defensive when you shouldn't be. You will discover that you will spend valuable time defending wrong premises. This is a fundamental truth especially in conversations that slide into arguments.

If you want to be assumed a great person, take time to ask about the things that matter in the person you are having a conversation with, their life interests, their beliefs, their family, and their kids. In any situation, lend a hearing ear, even if inside your mind, it just might be the greatest nonsense ever to cross your ears. This will leave the other person feeling good about them selves. You will be a shining star that every body will like to be with. In a conversation, its best to leave your personal views in the back ground, until you are asked. This is simple human psychology; we all like the sound of our voices. Let the other person rumble about them selves to you and you will make people want to be around you.

A good listener is a great conversationalist!

21 TIME

You and I have only 24 hrs in a day, 21620 seconds, if you like, and no more. Sounds almost a foolish statement to make, does it not? You have heard people telling you they are going to make sometime for something but its all empty talk. You cannot make time. Just look at your wall clock, that minute that has just passed cannot be won back, and cannot be stopped.

Of course in cosmic terms time is all a different ball game. If you could travel out there at speeds faster than light you will find your age mates upon returning a bit older than you! Well, we aren't cosmonauts, so we shall leave it at that, lest we get confused!

Did you know that you have an internal clock in your subconscious mind? It's always at work 24/7. Next time you want to put on your alarm to wake you up in the morning, remember to try your internal clock. Just tell your self before falling asleep what time you would like to wake up and presto, you will wake up exactly at the appointed time. For me, I long stopped using alarm clocks. Nothing beats the mind at time keeping! After all you can always stretch out to switch off your alarm clock, as for the mind once it has done its job, you will find it difficult to ignore it. You will toss in bed all day along without sleep supervening. Using mechanical time alarms in my view is a sign of poor self discipline. In the same vein never tell some one to wake you up; your mind can do that if only you give it chance to perform.

Time management is closely related to procrastination. Procrastination or putting off things you should do today to tomorrow is the greatest time waster ever discovered by man kind. Procrastination is a way of looking at the world upside down, for tomorrow may never come. Do not put off something you can do today to tomorrow, for you can never predict the morrow.

Learn to set goals for each day and stick to them. In fact, the best one can do is to write down your days, your weeks, your year's goals on paper. This will be a constant reminder to your mind of what it needs to be done. You might even mark off things as they are accomplished one by one. You will get tremendous satisfaction from this action. Each goal has to have a time limit simply because work, you should remember, always tends to expand to fit the available time. In short, always set dead lines for whatever task you have at hand.

Setting goals in life is a form of time management. For that matter, you need to have both short term and long term goals. These goals must be time specific and achievable. There is no point in telling your self you are going to fly to Mars next year! It aint gonna happen! Such a goal is time specific but not achievable, not realistic. They say running in circles is also running!

Set you priorities well. I once worked for a hospital where doctors started their day with a tea break! I had as the new head to really stump upon such time wasters, earning me a not so popular tug among the early tea drinkers! This also reminds me of an issue I had once with the head of Pharmacy in one hospital I worked who proudly displayed a notice of a" *work improvement"* meeting in progress caption at the front door of the hospital pharmacy at 08.30 hrs in the morning. Even a fool could tell that was poor time management, for at that hour in the morning, the queue of waiting patients was at its longest. Talk a about work improvement meeting!

Ill timed meetings a side. Aimless telephone chats and visitors are a thing you should always try to avoid. People who are failures in life want to pull every body else with them into the gutter. Reserve e- mail answering, telephone calls, staff meetings and visitors for the afternoon, if you are at any busy place of work.

That said let us learn from the Caucasians, they always make it a point to answer their mails. There is nothing more frustrating than not getting an answer to your mail. Make it a point to answer your mails. Don't make people wait for eternity for your answer. You only mess up your self! Unanswered requests and e-mails or sms' will just pile up.

Time is precious, use it well.

EPILOGUE

Well, how long were you at this small book? Don't you agree dynamite comes in small packages? Of course am no guru, so you might disagree on some of what you have just read. But at least you made the effort. Some things we surely agree on. Don't take it personal. Just pick a pen and say so, you might just help the rest of us. The world is not a boxing ring. Who knows, you just might crack the DNA code once again. Not all is known, we are listening.....!

Just look out for that pitfall ! Good luck!

ABOUT THE AUTHOR

Dr.Teddy Andrew Mulenga, born in 1958 in Kasama. Zambia had a humble poor beginning. He is a product of Zambia's premier secondary National Technical school of Hillcrest in Livingstone, along with Dr Nevas Mumba, who later served as Zambia's Vice President as well as High Commissioner in Canada.

. His pursuit of knowledge took him through the University of Zambia to the then Soviet Union, where he graduated in medicine in 1988, after sharing a room for seven years with his friend Dr. Joseph Katema, later to become a Minister in President Sata's Government.

Dr Mulenga, who speaks better Russian than English, prides himself in speaking other Zambian local languages and has widely travelled through out Europe and Africa. He is an avid reader and chess player. The Author spent more than 20 years working, as a doctor, in the small but vibrant country of Botswana. He is currently staying in the tourist capital of Zambia, Livingstone, a stone's throw from the mighty Victoria falls.Life,s Pitfalls is his second published literally work after the Sceptic book.

www.ingramcontent.com/pod-product-compliance
Lightning Source LLC
Chambersburg PA
CBHW060224290526
45789CB00003B/1402